Someone Else's Hunger

Someone Else's Hunger

Isabella DeSendi

poems

Four Way Books
Tribeca

Library of Congress Cataloging-in-Publication Data

Names: DeSendi, Isabella author
Title: Someone else's hunger : poems / Isabella DeSendi.
Description: Tribeca : Four Way Books, 2025.
Identifiers: LCCN 2025003852 (print) | LCCN 2025003853 (ebook) | ISBN 9781961897588 trade paperback | ISBN 9781961897595 ebook
Subjects: LCGFT: Poetry.
Classification: LCC PS3604.E75728 S66 2025 (print) | LCC PS3604.E75728 (ebook) | DDC 811/.6--dc23/eng/20250207
LC record available at https://lccn.loc.gov/2025003852
LC ebook record available at https://lccn.loc.gov/2025003853

This book is manufactured in the United States of America and printed on acid-free paper.

Four Way Books is a not-for-profit literary press. We are grateful for the assistance we receive from individual donors, public arts agencies, and private foundations including the New York State Council on the Arts, a state agency.

We are a proud member of the Community of Literary Magazines and Presses.

Contents

Last year I abstained
this year I devour

without guilt
which is also an art

—*Margaret Atwood*

****

ONCE, WHILE DISEMBOWELING THE CHICKEN

readying it for my lover's dinner, I remembered
my abuela slashing the rooster's throat. I was four.
Held the wet blade in my hand and cried. For days
the carcass hung like a cross over the red front door
until it shriveled and stunk, turned gray as dried petals.
Abuela said don't cry. She said be fearless & god-fearing
as any white man, so I became just like guajiros
carving the air with bright machetes.
At home, in school, in America, razors slept
in our socks like small slick moons, and hydrangeas
bloomed despite the heat while I became a woman.
For twenties, my tíos chopped weeds with green machines
spinning big metal mouths filled with hot blades.
You must praise the Lord with your body, Abuela said.
You must give yourself over as santeros do, without doubt.
At every ceremony for Dios, I held the white cloth
in my hands like a soul. Abuela slashed the bird
like a man unbothered. I thought the trick to surviving
this country was to be good or beautiful
or merciless like its people, but choosing didn't matter—
soon I'd be pinned on a bed like an animal
while someone else's hunger made a sacrifice of me.
Of course I tried to fight him off, but Abuela's birds
taught me when your arms are pinned behind your back

there's no chance of breaking free. *Across the neck*,
she motioned, *like this*, as she slid the blade
and prayed and ate. How can I forget
the hen's throat now—her pulse ablaze with fear
as I combed her feathers neat, placed her gently
on the altar. *Mira Isa, you must kill the bird.*
This is how we speak with saints.
This is how we prove our worth.
The knife was light. Blood ran through my hands
like a storm. I shouldn't have been surprised;
it was easier than I thought—replacing fear
with numbness, cleaving the bird's breast in two.
Stilled, her wings bent back the way my wrists bent
when he cooed me quiet, squeezed my neck.
Hands warm and strong as a god's.

POEM FOR ANOREXIA IN APRIL

Here was the body. And here was
the body rippled with nothingness
I couldn't rid. Like an animal caught
in the sewer of my life, I couldn't stop picking
at my skin, simple soft waste. Spring's pink garbage
strewn into the streets while petals performed
their daily adagio down the avenue.
I wanted to be like that: flat, punctured
with beauty even if it meant I would never
live again. Isn't that what I love most
about flowers? Their difference from us, reemerging
despite death. Their splendor–
perennial sufferance. I'll never forget
the shock of hibiscus: those big ripe heads
blooming diurnal against the dark edges
of the world. They know
what we don't: our lives are but a single shot
of exuberance. Then loss
and at the end of loss, what we couldn't unbury.
What carried us all the way.

Kevin DeLong
@kevindelong · Follow

I am embarrassed for my kids to watch this halftime show... what the hell. Stripper poles, crotch, and rear end shots.... no dignity. #SuperBowl #HalftimeShow shame on you Jennifer Lopez & Shakira

8:23 PM · Feb 2, 2020

178 Reply Share

Read 140 replies

Some people like to keep pigs as pets.
Some people are offended by JLo and Shakira
moving their bodies the way the ocean
has taught them to. *Rise, Fall, Sway. Rise, Fall, Sway.*
I will never understand how men can love
what they hate. So what we dip our hips—brutish, warlike,
gorgeous. In our countries, we don't have money
but we have mofongo, mythos, music,
mules—like us, the beasts of burden.
We learn to make beauty
from chaos, crashing. Like waves, we break
and break against. I am done explaining
why a woman's body is a woman's body.
The man who assaulted me says it was my fault
I wore a dress. I wish I could stand

on a stadium stage now with tulips in my hand.
Six-inch heels propping me up like a superstar or saint
while his small, stony eyes focus on my body
shaking like a hurricane, shaking like Persephone
did when she stood proud in her gown of darkness
and sang to her neighbors in the underworld:
Look at what you did to me
Look at what you did

AFTER A WEEK'S WORTH OF HARVESTING LOST DATA FOR A JOB THAT PAYS ME TO HUSTLE

in an office, the kind of office I grew up cleaning with my mother, I head to the salon for a manicure. The nail tech is new. Her apron reads *Alondra*. Alondra looks like my mother, has soft brown hands, weathered and kind just like my mother's. Together, we pick out the shade of red I want: *fever, sangria, or fury?* She asks. *Fury*, I say. Two white women sit next to us in silence buffing their nails into short pink moons. When Alondra and I sit, she takes my hands in her hands with a tenderness only daughters can understand and paints the color of anger or desire across the long lake of my nail, which hardens like a heart under bright manufactured light. The last time I sat this close to my mom in bright manufactured quiet, my hands in her hands, she was praying God would rid me of the disease that had me vomiting in secret at the lake behind our house where the water would congeal then break like dough under my body's simple rot. What spilled out: liquid like what leaks from a vase once tulips have wilted their way into death. What I miss most: the moment right after a purge. Always the miracle of birds arriving, like love, in a messy flurry. The way their wings beat furiously as they glided over the water, curious if any piece of me could be salvaged, was still good enough to be taken home to the other starlings to eat.

PORTRAIT OF MY MOTHER AS TIGER

—for Ileana de la Caridad Rodriguez DeSendi

Lord, I can't tell you why I do it. Only that
emptying myself was how I thought

I got clean. In eating disorder therapy,
they say food is a gift we deserve

but in Havana, where everyone is grateful
for their little bit of nothing, my mama ate

scraps the way tigers have learned to survive on bones—
by holding the memory of a carcass

like a loved one in their claws.
In America, my mama's claws

emerge, glint like cobalt in the sun. We clean
so many offices for rich people

our pockets shine with coins heavy as clouds
eclipsing the black tongue of the sun.

Now, Mama makes sure food is everywhere. Always
tienes hambre? In fact, just last week

in the middle of the night, I caught her
in the kitchen slicing an orange with her knife.

Like my mother, the tiger is barbaric, serene.
Like all wild things just trying to survive,

she has learned to break
things with her hands. Pray with her hands.

When a tiger kills, it buries the bones
in a bed of wet leaves, can never forget

the grave of its prey—a place it will return to,
the body that gave it life. Mama peels and peels

and the orange bleeds. *Will we ever return*
to our country, I ask? She picks the skin from its pulp

like a surgeon exposing the hardened husk of a heart.
Come closer, drink from me, her hands say.

I don't blame her for being desperate, deadly.
We'd be anything else in this world

if we could. Lord, forgive me but I lied.
When I said Mama's claws, I meant

her tears. When she asked *tienes hambre*
she was asking if I *have* hunger, if I possess it

as she does. Of course, I want to tell her—
isn't that what this insatiable void is?

Big as a country inside me,
grave I leave & return to.

AMERICA'S FIRST FEMALE MUSLIM JUDGE FOUND FLOATING IN A RIVER

—for Sheila Abdus-Salaam

In April we will find her body.
It is March. New York is gray, in-between
seasons like a heart undecided
between new love and loss.
No one knows why we found her
here, the dark truth of her body rising
up from underwater. Last night, while I was walking
down Broadway, some man across the street
called me a nappy-haired spic. Near the river
cherry blossoms ripen pink as wounds
against the sky. I can't believe
what we do to each other. Snow turns to fog
turns to dust over the branches. In ten, fifty, two hundred years
who will believe us when we say
the Earth was a hopeless chant, any man
was our captor. If I'm alive then I'm ashamed
of my mouth, silent as a thief. The man on my street corner
who begs for change, whom I choose
not to see. No one's life is the problem. The problem is a poet
can't always lay down in words a feeling
they know they'll never forget. When they say
I shouldn't feel powerless I agree, but many times

I've stood at the lip of this river
and wanted to crawl in. The M60 rolling past me,
kicking up muck. Maybe the problem
with the living isn't their sorrow,
it's that they're still capable
of violence. The feeling I can't forget is similar to flowers
falling quiet as knives
on the spring-punched street when they pull out
my body by the hair, and she lives.

HIPPOCAMPUS

—for Christine Blasey Ford

In the hippocampus, she says, they bounce around
like swallows dodging heavy blots of rain.

Like ivy, beauty makes her weapon
by making her like beauty: what men

can never hold. For the rest of her
life, every neural path is a coffin

of thought. When she sleeps
their beaks like laughter, drill deep

into her brain. I remember the year
after the first year. After numbness

when I would walk out
to the edge of a road, flat as a river

and whisper madly to the stars.
The well of my mind, darkening.

The highway's thick spine, heavy
as water against my back.

O God, if what divides
destroys then I understand

the mind, why it must live
separately from the heart.

Now, when I walk along the ocean
only the brutality of the tide. The moon

doomed in splendor, summoning
the water to rise and spin.

Like that, we tried to obey and love
the gentle crushing. Like that we fall

and fall. Now, how will we learn to hold a face
again when even orchids look like lips

bruised and sewn together? Yes, I tried
to love again, but when my man

undressed me, I felt the hands
of every man then felt

I couldn't breathe. No one was to blame.
It was spring. Buds were busy

mocking me, proving we could live
through many deaths. *How dare I?* I thought

but here's what no one told us:
every gentle thing will lose or lose

its body. That's the problem with surviving
again and again, as we have. Poppies will yawn

themselves awake, their bloodstained mouths.
One day you'll have to live.

HERODIAS WITH THE HEAD OF ST. JOHN THE BAPTIST

In your orgasmic stupor, you sleep
with a man's severed head in your lap

and in the man's head, a dry tongue
dead as a slug in late September.

In nature, brutality is law and there is nothing
more beautiful than the body of another

being whipped or chained or scoured because it means
that we've survived.

What else is ecstasy but the light
Cairo has chosen to paint you in.

Even the natural shadows that rest against
your eyes, soft and grey as unfurled sails

are at peace with the small wreckage
like a gift in your hands.

I know it's something stronger than sleep
which takes you now—

you're tired of enduring.
        Walking down Broadway, I imagine

mutilating every tongue that harasses the body
        I perceive as mine.

Herodias, teach me not to feel
        regret, to like the sound a neck makes

when it breaks, the blade cleaving
        clean through bone. I'd give anything to know

the pleasure you feel, his head
        resting where it is now. Show me. Put a knife

in my mouth. Leave a hole in my body
        big enough for you to touch.

ELEGY FOR TÍO LÁZARO

Because he was already dying, he figured
there was no harm in huffing through 2 or 3 cigarettes

in the early morning hours before my mother would wake—
the animal of his thin, brown body lassoed

to an oxygen tank. Because he didn't have papers
we had to drive two hours to retrieve the tank

from a discount store in Ocala
where my mom had to pay

out of pocket for air that would be filtered
from a rocket-ship shaped canister

into a tiny tube three times the size of a vein
directly into the soggy plastic bags of my tío's

stalling lungs just so he could drink cafecitos
& play crossword puzzles or the lottery

while we sat around in the kitchen
wondering how long we could keep him alive.

My mom was elbow-deep in dishwater
when the letter came

denying our appeal for his citizenship.
No, he could not get Medicare.

Yes, he would have to go back after living
50 years in this country. This country,

where, at 20, he learned to fix engines
in chop shops and likened himself

to a surgeon—saying any man with purpose could fix
any broken thing if he simply tried hard enough.

Entiendes sobrina? It's why God gave us hands.
Sometimes, I like to imagine him in the garage

surrounded by brutal heat and moonlight,
the broken chair under him barely keeping

itself together while he held metal chunks
in his hands like a heart, wondering where

it all went wrong, believing enough screws
            could put it all back. Of course, this was after he fell

in love with a woman in Kentucky,
            dreamt of being a local politician

and with that same American sense of disillusion,
            grandeur—discovered heroin: the god he'd worship

until he felt nothingness, & after nothingness
            the dull edge of sobriety, the death of his American wife

which meant the death of food stamps, which meant the death
            of a life that allowed him to lay on the roof of his car

while he smoked Marlboros and recited constellations:
            Andromeda, Aquilus, Ursa major, Ursa minor

which made him feel just as smart as the white men
            he swept for. Aren't our lives just simple constellations

made up of many deaths? Yes, someone in an office
            in a building in this country decided no, he could not

get medical care. No, he could not stay.
Two nights later, Lázaro woke from a dream

screaming aliens were coming to get him.
That their ship was hovering over the house.

The light so bright he couldn't see my mom's hands
as she helped him back to bed. The next night he died.

Milky Way: one answer on yesterday's crossword puzzle.
You can't tell me the dying don't know

when their time is coming.
The tip of the letter, still sticking out

of my mom's black purse like a cigarette
already flickering gone.

and the life I live in America claws me out from sleep.
        It's true that when I grovel the way Abuela has taught me
not to, Havana's doors open wide as the mouths
        of mis primas y mis amigas.

I know you don't want me to, Mama,
        but there are people we left behind
in our country. Windows painted the same blue
        I've seen peel from your skin

when a rough wind moves through you.
        Once, you said you felt smaller
than the corner of my ribcage where we stow
        the secrets of Santería. Dime, am I still pure

as the first tear shed from your father when he finally left
        the island, or are we rough, bleached, burned quiet
like your brother's palms scrubbing themselves into oblivion
        en la boca del mar? Don't push me away. When I braid

your thick hair, dark as a river, I hear the echoes of fifty niñitas
        praying at dusk. That's it, Mama. Next time you sleep,
tell the women in your dreams I've had enough.
        I'm coming with you. I want to peer through small windows.

I want my skin painted blue. Are you there, Mama?
        Mama, escúchame. Let me pray the words
you're tired of holding. Words that sink like sick doves
        in your hands: *Padre, Padre perdónanos.*

I DREAM OF HAVANA

and America claws me

Abuela has taught me

to open wide as

Windows

when a wind moves through you

Dime,

the first tear shed from your father

your brother's palms scrubbing la boca del mar

Don't push me away. your hair

dark as a river,

Mama.

tell the women

I'm coming. I want windows.

I want my skin

blue. Are you there, Mama?

Mira, escúchame.

What word won't sink like soft doves

except Father. Father, father, forgive us?

No, Father, I forgive you.

****

GROUP THERAPY VS. THE WESTERN WAY OF THINKING

"A woman is innocent until proven / angry."
—Evie Shockley

Apollonian thought is a Western construct
which teaches us that by naming a thing a thing
is to know the thing and by knowing it we attain power

or that's what they say in group therapy
when I'm handed a wet doughnut
and asked to name my attacker.

If it's true that we can't grip
a blade without shedding
our own blood, how can I say the things

he did? When I dream, I dream
I'm the goddess Kali—all sex & death
in her garland of skulls, the ego quivering

on its knees before me. Outside, I watch
the birds circle the air
until they don't. A red-breasted sparrow

chases her predator to its death.
        Again, they ask me to name him,
claim it. I won't. The group leader gets angry.

I get angry. The problem is so much
        is made from ruination that I can't stand
to recreate. Stars burning

through their bodies. New buds blooming
        through the rot of winter's wake.
I know they think a man who hurts

women is simply the product of bad love
        or pain, the way a storm is only rain
until it's coerced by darkness, wind. But look at history,

the way we laud the gods
        for chasing women to their deaths.
I'm done being desirous, taught to think

words will fill a void not even death
        can take away. *Say it* the girl next to me
whispers, but I don't want to give up

anything, and why should I? Of course
        a bullet hole will sing
if air is pushed through it, but tonight

I wear the garland. I hold his skull in my hand.
        Besides, I want the gods to suffer.
The Apollonian thought is dead.

AFTER THE BAR

I took the train and met a boy
who told me he wanted to take me home
and lick my pussy. He said I wouldn't have to
do anything except lie there—
lost, unfelt as new blear snow.

I still remember writing this:
lilies charred in summer heat
while I searched for some opposite to punishment
and light, like April, slipped through me
violent as cloudburst burning through fog

but even if I close the blinds, it's there.
Even if I tell that boy or that bullet
of sun they cannot enter, there's no mercy.
One will find its way, rest its head against me,
ask: *don't you want to be alive*

EVE'S PROTEST

Men insist I shouldn't use my body to conquer
them when men have been using me
to look at loneliness less directly. I solve
their endless wars; I'm a rack to hang
headless hats. Is it lunacy or resilience
when something breaks but we keep on
pushing through it? Becoming sacred
is an act of love or self-deceit. Just look at Adam
wrenching out his rib for me. Look,
all I wanted was someone I could show
my wretchedness to, someone
who would be there, loving. Or else, I wanted
to feel winter coming and not feel like an animal
who'd forgotten to wake up. Tell me,
what woman hasn't been tempted,
porous—only wanting
what she wanted. Do you blame me, Lord?
I'm only doing what you've done. Made a man
suffer then surrender before I let him love me.
I know I've said this already
but I mean it: Once, I was good.
Now, standing by the pier, the sky opens up
in late-night light like a scab unwilling to close
and I admit, part of me is still like you, Lord.

Some days, I'm tired. Some days, all I want is to
eradicate the earth. Instead, a man I love enters me
slow as light stabbing its way through to morning.
O God, don't refute this. I know your rage
is fueled by jealousy and your jealousy fueled
by sadness. You wish you could hold a body
like I do, and understand what I mean when I say
it was worth it. All of it. Yes, it was worth it.

HYMN FOR THE WICKED

It was bright when I walked into Mass. Light fell
through cold-colored windows, cut Christ's body

in half. If my hands weren't tucked between my knees,
I could let go of something. Catch the bird flying

around my head. What we learned: either we failed love
or love failed in us. Just look at what they did to you.

Hollow as the barrel of a breaking wave, your body
crushed and curling over. That you stood there.

That you took it. Now even the light is threatening
to slice its way through the nave, and the ageless

gnarled elms outside are limbs I want to nail
myself to. As for pain, it's worse when it's the hand

you know. Outside a hawk spears a lizard to an acacia branch
and I believe them when they claim any person's death

is always someone else's triumph. The wicked, we know,
are always redeemed. If I'm done with this world then I'm done

with arrows, doll's eyes, sea snakes: beautiful things
that are blameless, deadly. When I go, give me some direction.

Tell me where I should leave my mind: a newly budded thing
which cuts itself on every edge. Look, already my hands

are opening. Poisonous yellow dahlia
blooming quiet in the dark.

EURYDICE

Yoked as we were like a pair of oxen,
I carried for you what the cormorant carries
for its master: a promise to be fed.
Outside, the sky was gray as a blade
the day I opened up to sacrifice.
I never felt so understood as I did then
standing among the wood-pecked firs.
Having seen me scarce, now you say
you know desire. What we lack.
Don't turn toward me. Distance makes
you smaller. To see you standing there
is enough. You knew it would kill me:
watching the light gleam from your face
beckoning always, come.

WHAT I THOUGHT I KNEW OF LOVE

You're furious like a cloud of moths battering
against a bright hole in the night.

The hailstorm outside, your mind.
When you throw a bottle against the wall

the room disrupts into shards like the sky
when the sun first opens its bright gash

of an eye. After, you hold me. Death Cab
for Cutie plays on vinyl in the background.

As a cowboy first lays leather on a mare
teaching her to accept the weapon

that will dictate her life, so you taught me
the gentle language of hurt

we would speak. Sometimes, your teeth
on my ear. Or else, your palm like a thick whip

striking the sleek corner of my cheek.
Little bruises blooming blue. You know, I tried to leave

you once. Like an old mare, I even considered
laying down in the riverbed, but erosion

takes longer than sadness. Still, I tried
and tried to console you. Over coffee, a friend

said she pitied me, the torture my own.
I should've been embarrassed. I know

I moved through life like a plum-eyed sparrow
flying lopsided through the night

but I can't say I didn't like to suffer.
It was excruciating: the front door opening.

Your shadow in the doorway
eclipsing light from the smooth moon.

Then your eyes (always your eyes) soft
as an animal's surrendering. Your hands

on my face making a small shape like love.

SONNET FOR SKINNING DEER

Do what men have taught you. Stun me blind.
Drag me hog-tied under a fog-washed sky
until I hear only the river sloshing with rain.
Though it pulsed like an old scab, you were tender
with my heart. Shouldn't have felt pity for the hunter
but I did. See how it aches like a newborn
gasping, raw with life. First fur then blood pooled around us
like jasmine mid bloom. The smell of my death
ignited the air. There are pieces of me
everywhere. Clumped and scattering like beetles
in the gutter. Touch me; you love me flayed, hung flat
like a rug kicked clean. Go on then, do it.
What's stopping you. Your hands, sulking ghosts.
Your mouth, slick blade, already this close.

ELEGY FOR JOHN

—for John Rodriguez

The day they found my cousin in the woods
with a wound the size of a void in his head

they knew he was gone, but were unsure
if he'd fled his body yet.

On days like this, I wonder about the spirit.
Where it goes when the body declares

no more. We don't show John's face
at the funeral. No one wants to say it

but shrapnel has speckled his skin like rain
and the hole he left behind is still dark

and wet, deep as a lake. My tío cannot
contain his loss. He needs to know how cold it was

the night John trotted into the woods,
under skylight—

a deer hiding from what hunts it.
At the funeral home, a stranger tries to console us

says a bullet of that caliber
would have blown through him easy

like a god-sized wind.
As if there is any consolation in death,

we agreed. I thought I understood the mercies
of not being, but what do I know of losing my life

other than I wish something
that big would rush in, flood me.

Grief makes us ignorant, hopeful.
The shot keeps replaying like music in my mind.

First, the bullet blooming
through his brain like a minor scale unfurling

across the wet map of the sky.
Then, the particular silence

which always befalls tragedy. I'm angry
at the earth which continued reinventing.

John, gone. The new world, bright
and horrible after. Sunflowers: golden, everywhere.

ELISION

Now the nascent air of January
makes me ache. With it comes your

voice, warm as brass inside
a body slurred with ice.

When sorrow made clear as air the snow
that wind would have to lug, I was sure

I'd hear it all the time:
a sound as cruel as lonely felt.

Your mouth, a river dripping steam:
hot air rising in the culled-out cool.

That there was nothing left
to lose to silence, I considered grace.

I was stark as thin-boned birches
against the bloodless winter sun.

Back then, even a crow's caw reminded us
of flames—how they'd shudder

then unwind before being smothered by snow,
turn red then blue then ash then gone.

QUESTIONS FOR MARY

Rilke said the savior shouldn't have been carved
from Mary who was used up like a star
burning her way towards death. I only think of this

now, having seen a fox slink across the lawn's dew-drenched slope.
Like papers I toss into the fireplace, her body ignites
the entire yard. Wet red fur like first blood

against the snow. When I look at Michelangelo's Pietà
trying to see what Rilke saw, the wound appears
much smaller than I thought. The gash neither deep

nor wet as a gully. His ribcage punctured
neatly like an animal in a dark field. I don't care
what Rilke says. I want to be like Mary. Her hands sleek

with ash, abandonment. Or some days, I want to be the vixen,
nipples glowing swollen from a suckling's tender bites.
Tell me, without child, who decides if I'm soft enough

to be chiseled through? What worth does my body have if not
the chance to break open, sacrifice? I envy the fox's long body
fluttering, a scarf caught in the breeze.

Her pups buried beneath the earth in a heaven of light-soaked snow.
O Mary, help me to be selfless as a mother.
Whose head will rest in my lap

the way the slaughtered rests in yours? Only once have I held a man
that tenderly and it was only because he loved Rothko
and jazz and German beer as much as he loved fucking.

Now, I miss him sucking on my breasts
with a longing that wasn't dire. Any mouth on my body.
Just that simple, living need to be close to someone.

Tell me, what god would pick me? What else besides that void
would make me call the fox forward though she turns
her back and hides? I don't blame her. Instinct teaches

all of us the ways love can lead to ruin.
Of course, I want her pups to live, but I'm tired of praying
they might survive when I know they won't.

How could they? Winter is harsh here. This mother can barely feed.
On mornings like this, what choice do I have
but to sit in the yard and pretend I too have children

to tend to, something left of myself to give? O Mary, when that fantasy
doesn't work, and all I can hear is the caw of a longspur
echoing inside the trees, I try to imagine your face—

stoic but lenient as only good mothers can be.
It comes so naturally, this silence
filled with wind. All the clever ways

I imagine falling asleep in snow.

LAZARUS

The name I gave the mouse that made its home
in mine. The only thing I hated more than the way
it scurried like a shadow I never saw but sensed
was the beast I became because of it. Cowed, I knelt
on the floor like a saint searching for proof of its presence.
With my lover gone, this time for good, I learned to bait
and set traps. Needle springs into sockets
into mouse-sized holes. One night, I woke to a clamp
snapping shut and was relieved when I found the body
as if I'd done a good deed. Like wind, its breathing
stirred then slowed, a tiny heart valve closing.
The way its mouth hung open. The dark fur of its spine
bristled from shock, stood sharp as barbed wire.
I tried to feel sad, human
but I was teaching myself to let go. The spear of the trap
glinted with light dribbling in from the moon.
Paul says freedom is learning to let those who've hurt you
walk away, but this is how I know
I'm flawed: I wanted it to die. I kept dreaming
it would crawl into my bed, my mouth
the way a man I trusted did. For once,
I felt like the champion of my life.
But then the mouse's body rose—
sprung and lifted itself back to life. How could I be mad?

Even when it's over, it's never over. Don't I know
how it feels to be that close to escape, get graced
with one more shot? Look, God.
I'm still on my knees. Teach me to unfurl my fists.
Let my hands be hands again.

****

ARS POÉTICA EN EL MUSEO DEL PRADO

At the museum in Madrid, Pablo teaches us
about Titian's technique. Makes us move
around the octagonal room to witness
the ways in which a smear of white glaze
cast perfectly in the lagoon of Danae's naked armpit
highlights the shadows of her body
in greater detail from a distance. We move further away,
closer, then further again, noting how
she becomes incoherent, muted, then finally understood
depending on where you stand, the angle
at which you look. The room responds
to the brilliance, and it is brilliant, but I'm frustrated
that artists spend so much time articulating
details only to ask the world to step back
and see us through illusions we've created.
Why can't I just say I've lost someone I love—
someone who couldn't look past my flaws and now
I'm writing this stupid poem to ignore that simple fact.
Titian must've suffered reddening the velvet curtain,
carving out the edge between Danae's hip and thigh.
Light is the same as language. The technique of blurring
paint no different than metaphor or the sleight of hand
I just used when I said it was the artifice that bothered me
and not the fact that I am no different from the painter

having asked everyone for distance, thinking
my errors could be accepted if placed purposefully
in poems, objects witnessed from afar.
Even now, reader, this poem is only a fragment
of some wound I have had to admit, erase,
then dress up to show you. But I do like the painting—
Danae reposed, summoning. Her breasts pale
as a dove's underwing exposed in lambent light.
Pablo explains that in Danae's myth, Zeus sensed her desire
and came to her through a gold shower falling
from the sky. The truth is, what actually frustrates me
is Danae. Her autonomous pleasure. Her imperfect
body, beautiful. My wound is wanting to know
how it feels to be a woman that desired, desiring—
that even a god knowing all your flaws
would still shatter his world to reach you.

PEP TALK FOR MEDUSA

Don't let the girls with straight hair tell you
you're unlovely. Your kinky hair abominable,

pretty as a whip. Your hair hissing like rain
the sound shame makes when we sleep.

When I was seven, a girl touched my curls
and asked if I ever brushed them, if I had a mom,

where I was from. She meant who was taking care
of me. Who let me look this unruly. I told her

I too started girlish in the world
like poppies emerging feverish before

someone else's hunger made me venomous
as a woman. At a party in Bedstuy, a Latina

with thin, straight hair will say we're lucky
to be pretty, white-passing. She didn't know

my curls were brushed flat, buried
beneath a slick nest of a bun. Answer me, Athena.

In how many languages will I have to apologize
for someone else's gaze? Tell them it wasn't my eyes

that killed anyone, but simply the reflection
of their own dark staring back at them.

After the party, I went home and showered
then stared in the mirror at my brown skin,

black eyebrows, brown nipples, dark cunt
wondering if anyone could see me clearly

and to whom I was god, monster.

SELF-PORTRAIT AS A YOUNGER SELF

Though it hurt, I can't say I wish it didn't
happen. The memory, a sharp pulse lingering
like the best of my worst sins.
With time, even a crushed bird will sink
in a river going gone. In our breviary
every story is a story
about snakes. I straddle you and feed you
cherries from a bowl. Our faces like footsteps
becoming sad ghosts. Why can't we be perennial
instead of breaking open like blossoms
in the rough summer heat. Your daddy's daddy's
daddy said keep an aspirin pill
between her knees and you won't regret your life.
It's summer. The lake is dirty
and brown like my brother's long hair. When I dance
I dance to Charlie Parker. When I love I don't love
because I'm still doing it correctly. We can't help
but watch the trees shed their leaves
heavy as feathers. I'm worried
I might make love one day to a man and mean it. Or else
that I'll grow into my body and decide
it doesn't fit. When that boy throws me down, feels me
up for the first time, we don't know what to do

with my hands, his hands. My breasts, his eyes.
We thought the birds could fly. Could float.
We'd watch them drown forever.

THE PLAYBOY BUNNY LOUNGE

On a Wednesday night in New York, I ended up at the Playboy Bunny Lounge with a man much older than me. Think decades. I loved those girls. The way corsets clung to their bodies like shadows, unforgiving and tight as darkness. There was no competition. They were everything I wanted and knew I couldn't be. In their presence, I felt safe. Men were everywhere, but I understood I was only a woman and the bunnies simply more than. Like angels, they topped us off then vanished before we could find them, touch them. Like knives, their perfume sliced through blooms of smoke leaving the ghosts of roses in their wake. I envied and adored them. Always their breasts like sunrise stunning us. Always new and shining. Now when I think back to that night, I know it's when I learned what love is. Love: watching sad men pretend to feel the nothing they carry with them. Nothing: what women are always turning from. Maybe I don't know what distinguishes hunger from desire, but I know I want to be terrific as a bomb switch tripped—delicate, dangerous, glittering even if it means I must obliterate. After all, we spend so much of our lives trying to feel how we felt in that lounge. Uninhibited and unashamed; everyone felt wanted. Someday, I thought, these bunnies might be mothers. Someday, their breasts will dissolve into gelatin or ash. And the rest, we know, will wither—bald and bruised by grief or love. But that night, none of us were burdened by bodies. What I mean to say is a woman came alive in me and I disappeared. She lived.

REPRISE

Punchdrunk as bark being struck
by an ax: that's how your music broke me.

In yellow spotlight, smoke curled
around your face like woodbine climbing

the dark-skinned maples. Hearing you play
was like watching a sculptor carve bodies

from memory, wield the smoke-filled air.
What I loved most about your performance

was the way you summoned me to dance
like a snake being charmed. I was reckless

and porous, unspooling
myself in the bruise-blue dark. Isn't this how

it always re-begins? I let go. You reappear
without notice like a childhood stammer.

I know I shouldn't admit to this
but it's impossible to look away

from your hands, rough and sweating
on the gold-necked sax. When your fingers skate

across the instrument's body, rawboned
and gleaming, I think of the way your tongue

often sailed like a punt across me. Those altissimo
notes, sharp and bright as daffodils

unfurling, already beginning to dwindle away.
Like every solo you've ever played

or any man I've tried to love, we know
what dazzles disappears, shatters into silence.

At some point, I will learn to let you go
the way we let go of flowers

or the dead. Those we've carried & worshiped,
tended to & begged. Like them, you'll leave me

half-relieved & grieving, holding petals
that I'll shred. I'm scared of your absence,

what it will prove. I hope I do not suffer.

ELEGY FOR THE SAXOPHONIST

Turn off that Coltrane
    crooning from your iPhone and sleep.

Weepy and unhurried, eighth notes swarm through us
    slung drunk as transfused blood moving

through marrow the way a spirit moves
    through the new body

in which it must reside. Warm-blooded boy
    you were only warm for so long.

Like a graffitied wall in Brooklyn
    you were feral, death-stained, beautiful

in your vanishing. I hate that when I first heard
    you play, your music took me in

the way the swan-god took the girl. Handsome and lonely
    you dazzled like a god.

When you stepped on stage
    the way a ghost steps back

into its body, trying to kiss its lover
one last time, I thought of all the nights

I'd been backlit by a memory
that wouldn't fade away.

O my saxophonist, even if you hadn't come
to me then, I would've come

for you still. Loyal as an angel
sent to bring back the dead.

Once, a surgeon in Antarctica removed his own appendix
and I envied him. I don't trust the blood

inside me. With my hands that close to my heart
I don't know if I'd survive.

Come, I'd sing, bow down. Help me
unfold you, undress myself now:

unlace, unkeep, uncut.

VESPER

He'd finish his gig at the club
        then come over, handsome as a colt

in his sharply tailored suit. When I touched him
        I could still feel applause like rain thrumming

through his body. Gin on his breath like heat on the river.
        If you've ever loved an artist, you know they love

their post-performance high: dopamine lighting up
        the brain like sirens igniting a late-night sky.

When he's like this, he wants to drink. Then smoke.
        Then blow his air into my body

as if I'm made of brass. Which maybe I am.
        After all, don't I sing when a man puts his fingers

through me? Doesn't his tongue hunt down a sound I'll make
        once he's touched me

with tender mastery? The wild composure of him
        is what I'm grateful for when I hold his shoulders

in my hands. His eyes, sharp and blue
as absence, the initial sting of rain.

Once, we went dancing at a Nuyorican club
where we pretended to move like lovers

already knowing each other's bodies. When he sat on stage
with the band, what I loved most was his ease,

his belonging to the night—the way it made me feel
like I belonged to darkness too. At the end

of all the dancing, Tito drove us home
in his old Mercedes, bachata blaring

through the sunroof into Manhattan's mackerel sky.
Like the streetlights burning dimly

we were tired with our bodies, tired with music.
Even an instrument, which uses its hollowness

to express, to make—must break. Must sleep
then rediscover some new beauty every day.

SUMMER, AGAIN

meaning the city will wear her heat like beautiful hair—
thick and smug as grief—all over again. I've just turned
a year older, my best friend and I celebrate a new year
without loss. She's just booked her first real gig
on Broadway. On opening night, I slug
whiskey in a borrowed dress then slink into my seat.
She knows how much I love to watch her dance.
In the dark bars of Brooklyn, where music wallops
against the brick-boned clubs every Saturday, the bass pulsing
so loudly its absence will echo in our ears—
we dance, try to spin through the week's brief tragedies
clinging to us like sad lovers we haven't had the heart
to euthanize yet. If I'm guilty of unruliness, of using the music
to undo myself, my friend is coherent as a swan
shaking water from her body every time she turns
and bends, rebecoming something beautiful.
In the cab rides home, we laugh at guys, transient as ghosts
that tried and failed to kiss us goodnight. Sure, we dance
on them. We don't love them. We just love our bodies
on theirs, the pleasure we make. The way touching
someone else's skin makes us more aware
of our own. I tell my friend about the first woman
I danced with, how much I liked holding her
hips in my hands. She says her favorite thing about the affair

is that he loves her like a man should, doesn't treat her like a kid.
In a city where desire fangs anyone brave enough
to look its way, where to wear your skin openly must mean
you have nothing else worth living for, we realize neither of us
will sacrifice living for what the living do.
In July, she'll tell me she's pregnant
and cannot have the baby—but she wants to.
It's the first permanent thing she's done with her body.
Her life spent spinning minutes into tilts or manèges.
We know our need to be needed is innate, but the fantasy
happens anyway. Me: carrying Cheerios or cookies
or carrots in my purse. Her: dressing the baby
in purple tulle. For the first time in my life, I understand
my mother's grief. That night, when we walk home
through the park, I can't help but feel something
like shame since I don't how to care for her
while she weeps and weeps and carries her sadness
like a sunburn, everywhere. Now, even the early summer
rains, slow and gentle as mercy, cannot cool us.
In the meadow, just ahead, a little boy
is hand-fed crackers by his mother. What do we know
of a love like that, one that lasts beyond a season?
We know only this city. To take care of us, we have
only each other, the new bruise that will come

with winter's arrival, and the wind wiping away
the sweat from our eyes, taking from us
the awful heat that smothers then lifts then breaks.

SELF-HELP AFTER TINDER

The man in the text message says everything
he needs to say by not saying anything back at all.

As with poem-making, I'm forced to imagine
and therefore conjure every possible ending

until I arrive at something like closure.
Here's one I like best: us standing on a bridge

in Brooklyn like ravens resting against the dusk-floured hour.
The highway scaling the sky, purple

and wet as bougainvillea thriving
despite April's voracious rains–damn. There I go again

trying to make beauty from what is already
ruined. I wish you would text back. I'd tell you

if you stepped toward me now, I would let you.
This narrative would change. Yes, here's where

the readers would rage when I turn
from chaos, choose bliss. But here's the thing—

this is my poem, my life. And if my lover
wants to put their lips—wet and slow

as mud-soaked slugs against my neck
and tell me to come home so we can make love

and order ramen, well then—I will abandon
you, reader. It is more important that I live.

HEAVEN BIRDTHDAY

—for C.I.

When you called from the hospital in Escondido
the light was bright and sheer in New Jersey–
beautiful because it was blue and brutal, hard to appreciate

in the early morning. What scared me most about the call
was the absence of you I heard in that loopy drawl,
your voice dragging through the dry moat

of your mouth. Somehow during your manic break,
you'd managed to text me and say you were scared.
You thought you were being sex-trafficked

and could I come uncuff you and help you escape
the hospital before the bad men arrive to hurt you.
The nurse snatched the phone, tried to be empathetic

by explaining the ways Trazodone can make us delirious,
relax the prayer-soaked tongue. So I did what poets do
and turned you metaphor to soothe myself: imagined your mind

as a hallway of open doors, the symphony of drugs
slurring around your brain like snow
melting off a metal edge. Your mom explained

the trigger: you thought you were going to die
        on the same day as your brother, his heaven birthday
she called it—and how could anyone say you were wrong

for believing his unfettered soul would come back
        to reclaim you? Remember when we were 22
in Harlem and still believed in things like the soul,

spent all our time writing and smoking, wishing
        our neighbor would stop choking his wife.
We were young. There were so many things

we still wanted to have hope for. The efficacy of rat traps
        for example. Heaven. The soul's innate ability
to be saved. Even Manhattan, just an endless loop

filled with the coo of pigeons shitting
        outside our window and the splendor
of endless longing. Most days, we listened to Winehouse

or Willow. Other days, we wrote sonnets, poured
        pour-over, took pictures of frozen trees
as we tried to prove to our roommate

the corporeal existence of angels. One Sunday
        when you were hurting, you went to the police station
and returned with your brother's records. I found you

in your room, twelve hours later, just staring
        at the photos. You said it had been a long time
since you cried. You needed to know why

he stepped in front of the train instead of
        showing up to music class on a morning
much like this one: the light blue and sheer as a throat

cut cold. Everything too brutal to be beautiful–
        but I have no records to search through, Carly.
All I have are your poems and a certainty

that we spent too much borrowed money
        on that fancy MFA because after all that practice,
all that trying to wrestle words into thoughts into lines

into poems—poems which are, of course, just memories
        from muses, the mind's perennial dark stars—
you're still hurting and I'm still stuck

defaulting to tercets as a coping device
        hoping they'll help me navigate the wave of grief
I feel hearing you tried to drown yourself

days before we'd scheduled to meet,
        and all I'm ready to admit in this poem
is that I said I would help you escape

and I lied. I'm selfish. I need you here. Yes, the angels
        are with us, but they were not sent here for you.
It is not your heaven birthday. There are so many

more sonnets I need you to write. I need you to write.
        Please, make one more poem.
Describe for me the light. How blue was it?

How sheer was your heart? Tell me how the handcuffs
        were not actually restraints,
but a metaphor for a closed door

to which you eventually found the key.

****

ODE TO WOMEN IN SPRING

The concert of spring is beginning
and I'm trying to be better at forgetting
what's gone bad. The feminist manifesto I carry
with me says it's better to love men
than to hate, but when the Supreme Court overturns
Roe v. Wade, I want to erase myself like a tired star
shattering causing a messy galactic fire drill.
I know I said I'm trying, but I don't want this body.
Any body. I'm tired of burying
my rage in words. Let's just say the thing
this metaphor will try so hard to disguise: the animal in me
is not unlike yours or that man's or my mother's or the sun's
whose desire to devour is only obfuscated by the moon
or a simile which compares our hunger to the moon.
Our hunger, like the moon, waning then returning—
magnifying darkness the way it's always had to.
In time I'll become a woman, meaning I'll become
more like America whose nothingness
I've adopted is easier to look at than fear
or shame. Sometimes, on my lunch break, I smoke
on the stoop and stare at my hands, seeing
what the man at the bodega sees when he looks
at me counting quarters on the counter. How do I tell him
I hate his stupid orange awning more than I hate spring.

More than I hate azaleas which make me feel
like a girl who wants to celebrate new beauty.
Walking home, I pass a girl perfumed in liquor—
a lavender wine splatter staining the front of her
diaphanous dress. I want so badly to hug her
as she marches down Tenth, heels slung over her shoulder
like demons none of us can rid. Come here, I'd say
let's commiserate. Let's share the secrets we've learned
watching flowers bloom and wilt. They're not
unlike us, you know. Their gentle ruthlessness.
Their continuous dying. The way they persist in a country
that cherishes beauty, erasure, new beauty, slaughter.
Mostly, it's the way they stay receiving light
like any intolerable blessing, which always arrives
when we need it most. Afraid, yes—
but smothered by that dumb, crude hope
are still hungry enough to survive, to try.

MANHATTAN AT 26

Isn't it romantic how comfortable we've become
in Uber Pools, riding with strangers in the backseat
of a car? The highway rolls past us like promises
of the past. I'm thinking of all the possible ways
I can tell my future children I met their father
online. Streetlights like dreams or ghosts or ashes
flicker against the black map of the sky.
What do we really know about clouds—
the way they appear then disappear from
their bodies into the breath that feeds
the Earth? Walking down Lex, I play music
to silence the silence of my mind.
Nothing is romantic as April anymore
but I have discovered simpler loves. The queen
on my corner who spends her whole day shaming tourists:
You smell like a fucking asylum!
The taco truck parked in the same spot
on 1st Ave, kind and reliable as someone's God.
In December, when there is nothing beautiful left
except loss, I will learn to love words, the heaviest
thing a tongue can lift. For now, the breeze
is what it always is: thin and hot as a boy
who took me on a ride in his roofless jeep,
my hair whipping around us like rain.

Mostly, I am learning to see everything as numinous.
Even the metal high rises of midtown:
sterile and stern as a stepfather. Even the boys
that have abandoned me like an animal
leaving behind the bones of its kill, I love.
Without them, how would I know that picked clean
of myself, I could dazzle in the bright sun
that bleaches all of us into oblivion.

MANHATTAN AT 27

This year begins with the things we don't understand
and can't kill—murder hornets, stocks, the virus
that turned all of us into ghouls: little faceless
phantoms orbiting tiny rent-controlled tombs.
The stranger that was once my lover becoming
less strange to me again. During the month
when devastation teaches us how fragile
and inhuman we are, nothing feels
more salacious than sitting next to a body
I know I can't touch. In this almost-summer,
which undulates impossibly like the river's dark dress,
every flower is funereal, full with the kind
of quiet joy that follows grief's brief wake.
Why must everything good be obliterated
for us to understand its value?
In Queens, they're making space in hospitals
by wheeling bodies out in meat trucks.
My boss advises me to freeze my eggs
and I laugh—not wanting to admit
my uterus a tomb. When I speak with the doctor, I ask
If I get sick, will they fight to save me knowing I'm worth
only my life? This must be what Emily meant
when she described the formal feeling, the hour of lead.
Still, in the early evening, we do what we must:

trumpet from our balconies a sound that mimics pain or praise.
In the red hour that my ex-lover and I sit by the river
sharing tacos, we discover all the ways we've learned to live
with who we said we'd never be.
I just want a chance to be good, he says
folding his hands in his lap, away from me.
Me too, I say, trying to believe a version
of myself that exists in words. In the distance, a carousel
in Jersey spins endlessly on the water.
Its faint music like the cure, like the year we yearn for, still too far ahead,
but right now, in this moment, nearly reaches us, almost—

MILAGROS (SELF-PORTRAIT AT 28)

Alone in my studio apartment
in New York, I dance to Burna Boy
y reggaeton and post a video of myself online.

My mother calls to ask if I'm on drugs
because it's difficult for anyone to believe a woman
who lives alone might just be happy

shimmying in her skin the way the stars shake
and ricochet just before they burst
into the beautiful catastrophe of nothingness.

In true poet's fashion, I have to say I don't care
what they think. I have to build this analogy out of language
for you to believe I'm like the stars.

I know my ancestors would've danced with me
in quarantine because Cuba like NY is an island
where everyone is lonely

and everyone is grateful for their little bit of nothing
and joy is not earned but made. How else would we have bachata
if it weren't for sorrow, distanced lovers

finding each other's bodies
under the gold-hazed rim of a rum-shocked drink
which they sipped and spilled wherever they turned,

whenever they danced—when they dipped, when they groped, when they kissed.
When the congas, like familiar heartbeats, thumped like thunder.
Thumped as if to say: Step here. Breathe. Hold one another.

Haven't I been there? Been so hungry I was reckless. Felt so abandoned
in my body I let any man hold me so I could pretend
his hands were the hands of my first love

sliding down my hips? Listen, all I'm trying to say is this world feels
like an incomplete phase of the moon, minus beauty.
All I'm saying is what my people in the Caribbean

have always known to be true: that a slick melody strummed against
a summer sky rhythming is key to setting you free.
Of course when Burna Boy blares, I'm a hurricane spiraling.

Of course tocar means to make music and to touch. When I strum
the impossible instrument of my skin, I'm a cello humming light,
doing what I must to shake the night sky from my bones.

My therapist's therapist says it takes years to shake a trauma from the body
but here's what suffering—I mean, the combustive bodies of stars
have taught me: burning is the only way

some of us can get clean. The problem is sometimes I forget this.
And when I start to feel this way, when I begin
to face the hard truth

that I might not ever be deeply loved by anyone
ever again, that it might just be me and this brown body
alone forever in this home, well, I turn on my music

and let the bass snake up my leg because I still love the ruckus it causes.
The chaos of my hips like prayer, releasing something.
Like prayer, revealing my sloppy, ineffable heart to the gods.

O reader, how else can I admit this? All I want is to be held.
All I want is for you to come closer
and dance with me. Yes, dance with me

right here, right now in this shitty kitchen light
and see if you don't feel free once reminded
that our fabulous, infinitesimal lives

flickering flickering flickering
are just like the stars: bright musical miracles
that make it ok to say we are.

ODE TO WEIGHTLIFTING

When the men crushing bicep curls stare at me
loading whatever weight I have chosen
to suffer through today, I can tell they don't believe me
when I position myself under the iron yolk
like the beast the world has taught me to be.
They still think the plates weigh more than the burden
of a body I've been carrying all these years.
How do I know they hate to see me do it?
Because I've seen that look in my own eye
staring down at this body—what she couldn't be.
What she is. When pink callouses bloom across the fields
of my palms, evidence I've endured, I remember
what being crushed has taught me: I will always adore
the gentle animal of my body. This lonely soul-machine.
Now, what won't I yearn to push through? What fire
won't I undertake? Under the bar there's no shame
or feeling sorry. Just the woman inside me
alchemizing, sanctified. Just my body made mule.
How do I admit the pleasure I feel
as I pull and carry and push and drop?
That with an anchor tethered to my chest or back
I believe I am autonomous. Gentle as a bullet.
Powerful as memory. God-sent like the moon.
That even on those days when I try to lift myself from the floor

only to find the tiny motor inside me won't start—
or else, that it wails insanely like a child being left alone
for the first time—I know I'll still go on because
whenever I am edged toward the brink
of being shattered or stripped or eradicated
the way birds are every winter, the way women are
every year, I know I am breaking and breaking
as living requires we do—but sometimes
in the breaking I am bettering
and in the bettering I am free.

BROOKLYN AT 29

At the reading in Brooklyn, in the loft
with rooms as vast and gorgeous, numerous
as arteries, there is a rooftop bedazzled
with string lights where we sip free champagne
and ease under an easy sky Septembering.
When the headliners read, my friends coo
and laugh and feel so deeply, I'm proud
to know and love them. After Tawanda reads
from *Please make me pretty, I don't want to die*
all I can think about is my mother
and briefly, the country we left behind.
I'm 29. Like Tawanda, I'm trying to prove
to myself or the world that I'm worthy of writing,
but I'm still busy learning the forces beyond desire
that make me want to stay alive. Ask any poet:
this is how beauty works—some hollowness
or tragedy always scarring the blossoms blue.
The hole disaster leaves behind: evidence
that what we've lived through is truth.
Truth: a poet's way of making something useful
out of fire, rain, lust—any sunken, lonely ship.
But tonight, only the smell of rosemary from Joe's
floating down North 1st. Only the blackberry currant
I lick off the lip of my red cup while we watch

the crisp stars glimmer like every perfect break
in every perfect poem. We clap. Cat rests her head
on my shoulder. Phil laughs with a generosity
only angels possess and my lover is home,
has messaged that he's waiting with takeout,
waiting for me to come home so he can play
with my hair until I fall asleep, and I realize I am happy.
I am so fucking happy. There is no other way to say it.
I must go on. I must go on. The poem must end like this.

THE BUFFALO

Spring will come and with it the audacious dirt
and corrugated banks reliquified blue. Upstate,
where I met your father for the first time, we mazed
our way through a snow-barreled zoo
confettied with funereal trees—final markings
of winter. Early in this still, I felt new
when you placed your hand on my neck, soft
as a moth's wing wind-ripped, resting,
having awakened and fed, full with dark.
This feeling was the opposite of dusk beginning
to lay itself down like a ghost in the long grass.
In a knot of red branches white birds
nested, made me think of blood and skin,
my mother's disease, and the horrible truth
that all our parents will die. I try to hide
the thought from you but you've already learned
how desolation unravels me. Things like
this sky slurred blue by winter's music
aiming its harshness everywhere. Things like
the buffalo which has exited his den
and walks over to where we stand, nuzzles
our palms pressed flush against the gate.
It was as if I suddenly understood
my life when that creature stepped into

the world and kissed the soft side of my hand.
Such terrific beauty confined in that ridiculous cage.
My disbelief, my pity. His tenderness despite.
What else could be more miraculous
than an imprisoned thing that chooses gentleness,
still yearns to be touched? At any point,
the buffalo could change his mind, run through
the hole-pocked fence and obliterate us.
I turned to you and said I hoped we would be
this trusting forever. I wanted to set him free.
We were foolish, of course. We knew that.
You moved closer to the gate, pressed your face
against an opening in the slats the way a saint
might approach a god he's never met
but trusts, and you touched his eye
with your eye. You were not afraid.

MY DEATH URGE IS STRONG (SELF-PORTRAIT AT 30)

Kait says my death urge is strong—
        that's why I try to sabotage my life.

Far out on the river, boats float from harbor
        to harbor like lovers becoming strangers

becoming lovers once again
        and all I can think about is distance, my mother

and the hunger she carried with her
        before she became American, hunger that spreads

in me like juniper erupting all over the park
        the winter I decide I can't breathe, don't eat.

I'm in a new city now, but I'm not lonely. Kait was right
        about my urge but we're not friends anymore.

October again, the engine of summer stopped
        by the galloping trance of an impossible cold

light and unshakable as the music
        of one hundred blue wings

humming like soft machinery
in my bones. I thought by 30 I'd stop looking

at my body as a wind-ripped metaphor—
or would at least have learned to love

my ruinings the way a child loves collecting pennies—
worth something because they unburied them.

Worth something because they're mine.
Instead, I order oat lattes every day of the week

and practice laying sentences down in stanzas
like bodies lying on a bed. These days, I am only writing

to understand the character of myself as an attempt
to have grace when I fail me.

In here, there is a version of me that never felt
shame for helping my mom clean offices for cash.

The light is dewy, cinematic. I am inarguably holy
and never lonely, never cruel. In here, I can recite

the name of every film in Timothée Chalamet's
repertoire even though Kait told all our friends

that I'm an indie film poser. I don't care.
This is what life is: intimacy, chance, the thrill of so much

beginning new and so often always its end.
At the beginning of my mom's new life,

a photo was taken of her blowing kisses
toward the shore the day she left and never looked back.

I miss the friends I've lost to age, small griefs, love.
In poems, I can remember them.

In poems, I can believe the person I say I am
in a story I invent that goes like this: Bella waits

by the water when a dog, loose from its leash,
runs up to her ecstatic, demanding to be acknowledged

as the living often do—yes, I decide
the plot will start here: the animal bounding toward her.

Its face held between her palms
    the way only strangers' faces can hold the mystery

of one another. For just a moment, this trust.
    Eyes linked having understood

the wildness that rests between them.
    But before you think of me as hero, know this:

I knew my mother was hungry
    and I still took food from her plate.

The dog returns to its owner as it must.
    I don't save anyone

but I blow kisses to all the strangers
    passing by me on small boats. Nothing else

but a blue sail on the water
    growing smaller in the distance.

Acknowledgments:

The Adroit Journal, *Brink*, *Brooklyn Poets* Feature, *The Grief Diaries*, *Leveler*, *Narrative*, *Palette*, *POETRY*, *Poetry Northwest*, *Rattle*, *Small Orange*, *Two Peach*

"Herodias" *The Ekphrastic Review*, republished by *Palette*

"Elegy for Tío Lázaro" published by *Rattle, r*epublished by *2024 Best New Poets* anthology

There are so many people without whom the poems in this book would not be possible–my life would not be possible.

First, God who gifted me this singular, beautiful life. Talent is never enough. Every beautiful and complicated thing I know about surrender, I've learned by surrendering my life to Him.

To my parents who have shaped me into the woman I am today, I have endless gratitude. Mom, your tenacity, selflessness, hustle, fire, and belief in me make up the accelerant that keeps me going. You are my north star, always. Thank you for gifting me a love for language and reading. I will spend the rest of my life arranging words to try to fully express my gratitude for everything you have done and sacrificed so that I can chase these wild dreams. Gracias, Mama, por todo. I love you to the moon and back. Dad, your humor, introspectiveness, kindness, and ardor for music and all things 80s is a forever lighthouse that illuminates my dark. Thank you for the gift of joy and for teaching me how to think deeply. To my brother, you keep me laughing and humble, homie. Thank you for always having my back. I hope your sissy has made you proud.

To my partner, Matt, none of anything I have set out to accomplish would be possible without the love, safety, and support you give me. Thank you for being my best friend, my cheerleader, and for teaching me how to trust men again. Your kindness, patience, and green eyes are what keep me anchored in every storm. I look forward to being your wife and to writing poems beside you in bed for the rest of forever.

To my dog, Ziggy, who has taught me what it means to be responsible for a life and love in a new, expansive way. Mama loves you, Moochie.

To Lavilla and Douglas Anderson School of the Arts who first helped me develop my chops and introduced me to poetry, I will forever be grateful for the education you gave me. Thank you for taking all of your students seriously, and for showing us what it means to be a writer.

To my mentor at the University of Florida whose brutal edits constructed the barometer with which I measure my poems today, thank you for teaching me how to revise, how to construct a line, and ultimately, kill all my darlings. Your mentorship during my collegiate days was invaluable.

To Columbia University and New York City—you provided the space to take writing seriously. To create and make mistakes. Workshopping with all those brilliant minds made me a better poet and teacher, and I am so grateful for the caliber of education I received while in your studies. New York, you are a forever teacher. Thank you for feeding my soul.

To my ancestors, who came from Cuba with nothing, who made new lives in a country that was not easy to survive in, thank you for your faith and audacity. You carved a way for me to exist in this world and I will never take that for granted.

To my friends and peers, thank you for being my second family, for helping me carve these poems into what they are today. I couldn't possibly name everyone here, but please know I love you all so dearly. Thank you for your love and guidance.

To all the editors and journals that took a chance on me and published the poems that appear in this book, thank you for giving these pieces their first homes. Every publication was an affirmation that I could really make a life of this.

To the people who have wounded me, broke me, loved then unloved me–I say thank you. You taught me resilience and forgiveness, which are key to being an artist. Your injuries made me grow and taught me what a useful energy source rage can be, and I am all the better for it.

To me–Niña, thank you for continuing even when you didn't know how, or that you could. You are resilient, strong, beautiful, flawed, but I am so proud of you, my girl. Keep going. Be happy. Don't ever stop writing. Don't ever let go of your light.

About the Author

Isabella DeSendi is a Latina poet and educator whose work has been published in *POETRY*, *The Adroit Journal*, *Poetry Northwest*, and others. Her chapbook *Through the New Body* won the Poetry Society of America's Chapbook Fellowship, and was published in 2020. Recently she has been named a New Jersey poetry Fellow, was included in the *2024 Best New Poets* anthology, and has been named a finalist for the Ruth Lilly Fellowship and *Rattle*'s $15,000 Poetry Prize, among other awards. Isabella has attended Bread Loaf Writers' Workshop, the Storyknife Writers' Residency in Alaska, and holds an MFA from Columbia University. She currently lives in Hoboken, New Jersey.